COME ALONG . . .

for a new adventure. THE A B Q BOOK is not like any other
book you have read before. It takes you into the lives of Bible-
time boys and girls and shows you how they lived and what they did.
If you like to explore with interesting questions, you'll like THE
A B Q BOOK. Look at each picture, find out what it is, then ask the
question about it. Of course you won't know many of the answers!
But it's fun to guess. Then look up each answer in the back and
read about it. You'll find a new adventure in learning Bible from
A to Z.

A WORD TO PARENTS AND TEACHERS . . .

THE A B Q BOOK is designed to meet the interests
and needs of children of many ages and abilities.
Within THE A B Q BOOK there are three learning levels. It is important that you understand
these as you work with your child.

1. *Picture-reading level.* Children of almost any
age or ability enjoy looking at pictures and as-
sociating words and meanings with them. The
very youngest child may wish to do no more
than "read" these pictures. By doing this, he
will become acquainted with many important
things in the Bible.

2. *Question-and-answer level.* A more advanced
learning level uses the question-and-answer
approach. In THE A B Q BOOK, children
guess which answers are right, without the
pressure of feeling that they should already
know those answers. Learning is fun, not a re-
quirement. After the child has guessed his answer, he will look in the back to see how well
he did.

3. *Supplementary-study level.* When a child has
discovered the correct answer in the back, he
will enjoy reading more about that answer.
Through these three learning levels, the child
is led gently into a study of important Bible
information from A to Z.

THE

by V. Gilbert Beers

Illustrated by Alla Skuba

THE SOUTHWESTERN COMPANY

Nashville, Tennessee

BOOK

angel

ark

altar

alms

A

Abraham

adder

1. If I had been on Noah's ark, I could have seen an
   a. airplane   b. antelope   c. ape   d. ambulance
2. If someone had given me alms, he would have given me something
   because
   a. I worked for him   b. I sold him something   c. I was poor
3. If I had lived with Abraham, I would have lived in
   a. a tent   b. an apartment building   c. a house trailer
4. If I had seen an adder, I would have seen a
   a. worm   b. snake   c. machine that adds numbers
5. If I had used an altar, I would have
   a. sat on it   b. wore it around my neck
   c. burned meat on it to worship God
6. If I had seen an angel, I would have known that he came from
   a. a far country   b. a priest   c. God

1. If I had poured milk from a bottle, I would have held
    a. a glass jug   b. a cardboard carton
    c. an animal skin sewed around the edges
2. If my mother had taken some oil from a barrel, she would have
   taken it from
    a. a big wooden keg with iron hoops around it
    b. a big clay or stone jar
3. If I had been Benjamin, I would have had a brother named
    a. Joseph   b. Lazarus   c. Paul
4. If I had lived at Bethlehem, I could have seen a baby named
    a. Moses   b. Esther   c. Jesus
5. If I had seen a basket made of bulrushes, it could have held the baby
    a. Jesus   b. Moses   c. Abraham
6. If I had found a box, I would have found a
    a. cardboard container   b. small clay or stone jar

box

bottle

Benjamin

barrel

bulrushes

Bethlehem

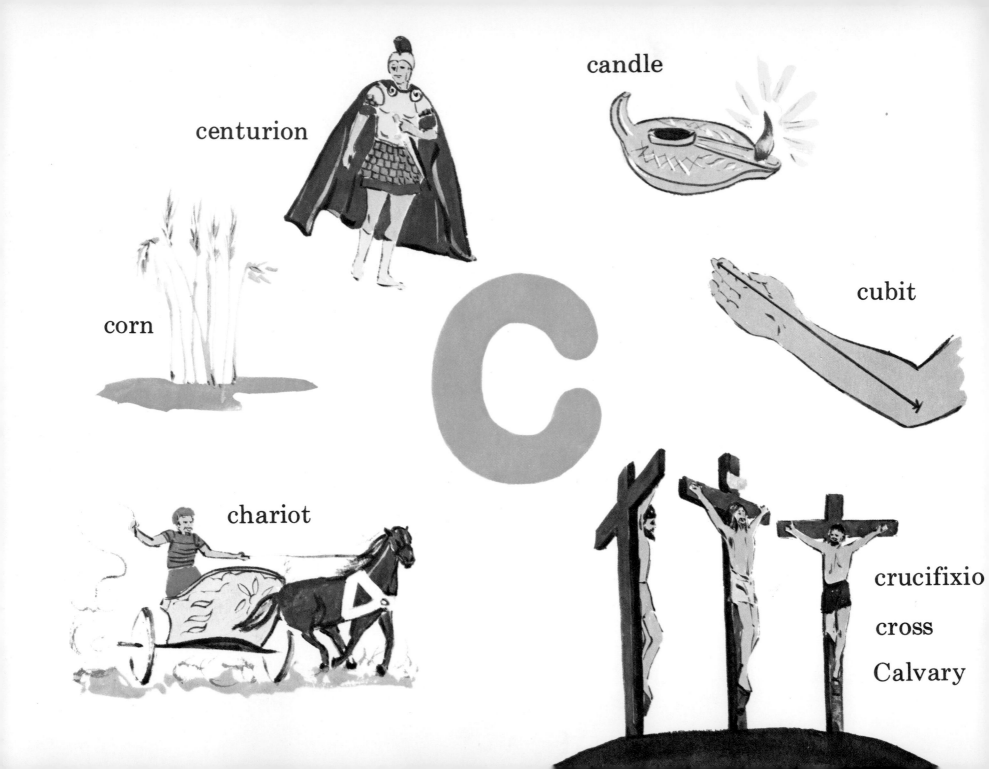

centurion

candle

corn

cubit

C

chariot

crucifixio

cross

Calvary

1. If I had lit a candle to put in my room, I would have
   a. put a match up to a candle made of wax
   b. poured oil into a clay lamp and put some fire on the oil
2. If I had wanted to measure something that was a cubit in length, I would have
   a. Used my arm to measure it
   b. Used a tape measure or a yardstick or a foot ruler
3. If I had been at Calvary, I would have seen
   a. the crucifixion of Jesus on a cross
   b. a group of men fighting on horses
4. If I had ridden in a chariot, it would have been pulled by
   a. oxen   b. horses   c. a truck   d. a motor in the front
5. If my father had grown some corn, it would have been like
   a. our popcorn   b. our Indian corn   c. our wheat or barley
6. If a centurion had come to visit our house, he would have been
   a. a temple priest   b. in charge of the community center
   c. a Roman soldier in charge of 100 other soldiers

1. If my father had worked to get a denarius, he would have worked all day to get a coin worth
   a. about 16¢   b. about $1.60   c. about $16.00
2. If I had read the Decalogue, I would have read the
   a. Ten Commandments   b. first book of the Bible
   c. Golden Rule
3. If I had seen a dog, it would probably have been
   a. a pet that people kept in their house
   b. an animal that lived in the street and ate garbage
4. If I had met a disciple of Jesus, he would have been someone who
   a. followed Jesus   b. quarreled with Jesus
   c. had been healed by Jesus
5. If I had read an epistle, I would have read a
   a. letter written on a scroll   b. book printed in Jerusalem
6. If Eunice had been my mother, I would have been
   a. Timothy   b. John   c. Philip
7. If I had been in the Exodus from Egypt, my leader would have been
   a. Noah   b. Moses   c. Joseph

dog

epistle

Exodus

Egypt

D E

denarius

disciple

Eunice

Decalogue

fan

frankincense

farthing

firkin

frontlets

flags

fetters

1. If I had seen the frankincense that the Wise Men gave to Jesus, I would have seen some

    a. resin from a tree   b. flour to make cakes   c. gold jewelry

2. If my father had worn frontlets, he would have had

    a. buttons on his cloak   b. a little pouch on his forehead with Bible verses in it

3. If I had seen fetters, or chains, on a man's feet, they would have been there

    a. to keep the man from running away

    b. as part of a Bible-time game

4. If someone had shown me some flags, he would have pointed to

    a. some flags of Israel   b. some marsh grass

5. If someone had told me to drink a firkin of milk, I

    a. could, for it was only a pint

    b. could not, for it was about ten gallons

6. If my father had wanted to earn a farthing, he would have had to work

    a. no more than an hour   b. at least a day   c. at least a week

7. If I had used a fan, it would have been to help

    a. cool my house   b. take chaff from my grain

1. If I had used a glass, I would have
   - a. drank milk from it   b. looked at myself in it
2. If I had fought Goliath, the giant Philistine soldier, I would have been
   - a. Daniel   b. David   c. Saul
3. If my mother had asked me to grind some flour, I would have used
   - a. an electric grinder   b. two big stones   c. my teeth
4. If I had seen my mother glean, she would have been
   - a. gathering grain left in the field by harvesters
   - b. washing clothes on some rocks
   - c. brushing her teeth with toothpaste
5. If I had met a Gentile, he would have been
   - a. a priest   b. a Jewish ruler   c. someone who was not a Jew
6. If I told someone the Gospel, I would be telling the good news about
   - a. Jesus   b. something I had done   c. my country

Gospel

glass

Gentile

Goliath

glean

grind

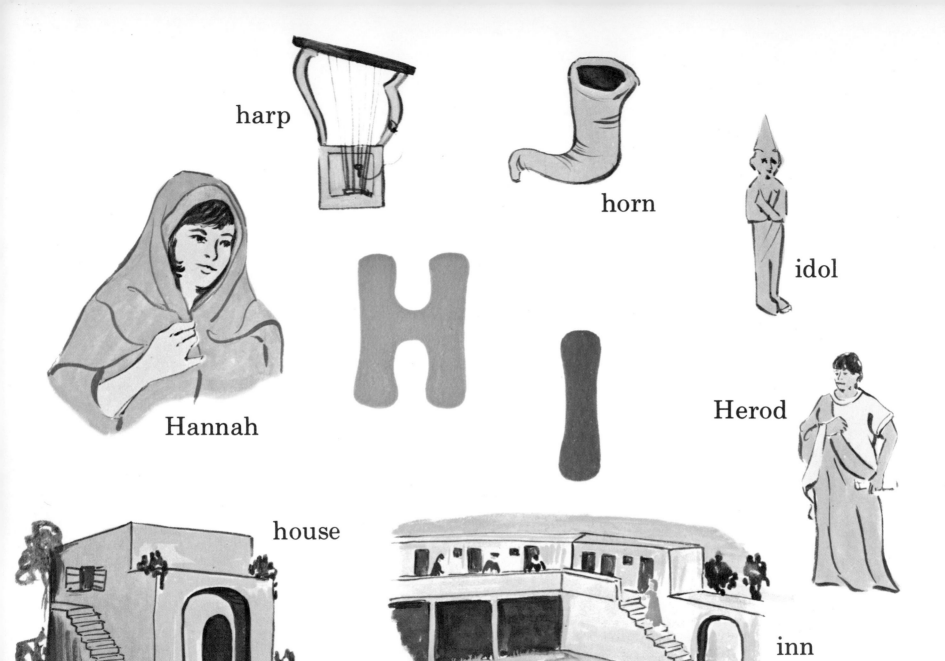

harp

horn

idol

Hannah

Herod

house

inn

1. If I had used a horn, I might have blown on it, or
      a. put it on my chariot   b. put oil in it
2. If a neighbor had owned an idol, he would probably have
      a. worshiped it   b. eaten it   c. slept on it
3. If I had known a man called Herod, he would have been
      a. a ruler   b. a slave   c. a royal barber
4. If I had lived in a house, it would have been made of
      a. glass and steel   b. stone or mud bricks   c. boards
5. If I had stopped at an inn, it would have been to
      a. get a hamburger   b. stay all night
6. If my mother had been Hannah, I would have been
      a. David   b. John the Baptist   c. Samuel
7. If I had used a harp, I would have
      a. speared fish with it   b. fought with it   c. played music on it

1. If a soldier had thrown a javelin at someone, he would have been
    a. playing a game with him   b. trying to hurt him
2. If I had been a Jew, I would have been
    a. someone in Abraham's family   b. someone who lived in Judea
3. If I had seen kine, I would have seen
    a. pigs   b. cows or cattle   c. kangaroos
4. If my mother had used a kneading bowl or trough, she would have been
    a. mixing dough for bread   b. washing clothes
    c. knitting
5. If I had heard the name of Jesus, I would have known that it meant
    a. son of Jesse   b. Savior
    c. someone who lived in Jerusalem
6. If I had been someone's kinsman, I would have been his
    a. king   b. friend   c. relative

Jew

javelin

Jesus

J K

kinsman

kine

kneading trough or bowl

lamb

leper

latchet

locust

lamp

L

Last Supper

1. If I had seen someone burn the meat of a lamb on an altar, I would have known that he was
   a. worshiping God   b. roasting meat for a party
   c. getting dinner
2. If I had been a leper, I would have had a disease that made me
   a. look like a leopard   b. have sores and white spots
3. If I had seen a locust, it would have been an insect like a grasshopper that ate
   a. cattle   b. crops in a field   c. people
4. If I had been at The Last Supper, I would have seen
   a. Jesus and His disciples   b. Jesus and the Pharisees
   c. Noah
5. If I had tied a latchet, I would have fastened
   a. something like a door latch
   b. something like a shoestring
6. If I had used a lamp, I would have
   a. turned on a light switch   b. lit it with a match
   c. filled it with oil and lit it with fire

1. If I had used a millstone, I would have been
   a. playing a game   b. fighting in a battle
   c. grinding flour from grain
2. If I had earned a mite, I would have owned the
   a. smallest coin   b. biggest coin
3. If I had picked up manna to eat, I would have had something like
   a. bread   b. french fries   c. roast beef
4. If I had seen an animal using a manger, he would have been
   a. sleeping in it   b. drinking from it   c. eating from it

5. If I had seen a man using a mantle, he would have been
   a. wearing it   b. lighting a lamp with it
   c. cooking his dinner with it
6. If I had seen the Messiah, I would have seen
   a. Moses   b. John the Baptist   c. Jesus

Messiah

millstones

M

mantle

mite

manger

manna

 Nicodemus

 Naaman

 New Testament

 Noah

 Nazareth

1. If I had met Naaman, I would have seen a
      a. Syrian army general   b. Jewish high priest
      c. disciple of Jesus
2. If I had worked for Noah, I might have built a
      a. chariot   b. pyramid   c. big boat
3. If I had lived at Nazareth, I might have known a boy named
      a. Abraham   b. Jesus   c. Isaac
4. If I were reading the New Testament, I might read a book called
      a. Romans   b. Chronicles   c. Psalms
5. If I had talked with Nicodemus, he might have told me about his
   visit with
      a. Jesus   b. Paul   c. King David

1. If I had used some oil, it would have come from
   a. a filling station   b. an oil well   c. some olives
2. If I had picked some olives, I would have picked them from a
   a. bush   b. tree   c. vine
3. If I had bought an omer of flour, I would have had about
   a. a pint   b. a half-gallon   c. a bushel
4. If my mother had heated her oven, she would have
   a. turned on the electric stove   b. turned on the gas stove
   c. put some fire in a big clay stove that looked like a jar
5. If I were reading the Old Testament, I might read a book called
   a. Obadiah   b. Philemon   c. Jude
6. If I had given money at God's temple, I would have
   a. put money in the collection plate when it was passed
   b. put money into a tube that looked like a trumpet

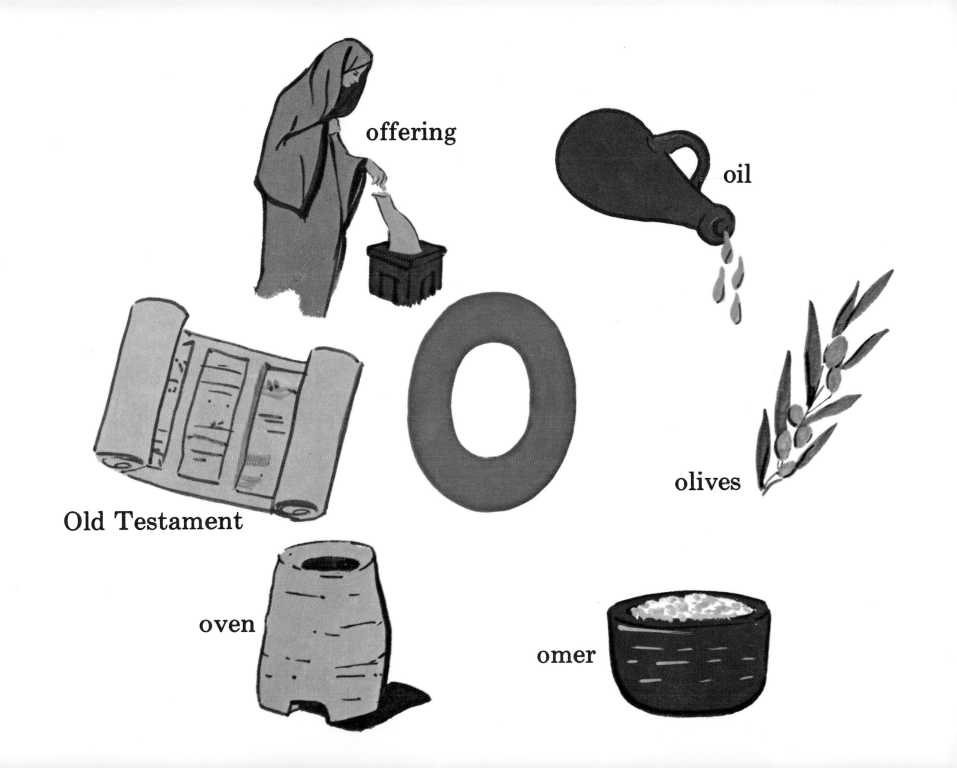

offering

oil

olives

Old Testament

O

oven

omer

prophet

pottage

plumbline

Pharisee

P

penny

plow

1. If my mother had made some pottage, she would have made something like
   - a. soup   b. soap   c. scraps put together for pigs
2. If my father had used a plumbline, he would have been
   - a. picking plums   b. building a wall
3. If I had earned a penny, it would have been worth about
   - a. 1¢   b. 16¢   c. $1.00
4. If my father had used a plow, it would have been pulled by
   - a. a tractor   b. horses   c. oxen
5. If I had met a Pharisee, I would have seen a man who was
   - a. a shepherd   b. a religious leader   c. a disciple of Jesus
6. If a prophet had come to eat dinner at our house, he would have talked about
   - a. the work he did in a bank
   - b. his eighth-grade class at school
   - c. God

1. If I had met a rabbi, I would have seen
   a. a Bible-time rabbit   b. a mad dog
   c. a religious leader or teacher
2. If I had used a rod, I would have been a
   a. shepherd with a big stick
   b. plumber who cleaned out drains
   c. racing driver with a fast car
3. If I had known a Roman, he would have been
   a. my slave   b. my religious leader
   c. one of the people who ruled my country
4. If I had used a quiver, I would have
   a. taken my temperature with it
   b. put arrows in it
   c. worn it on my head
5. If I had known a queen, she might have been
   a. Ruth   b. Hannah   c. Esther

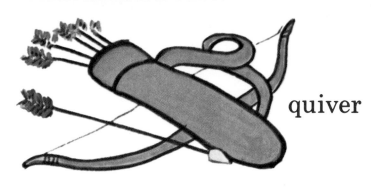
quiver

rabbi

queen

Q  R

Roman

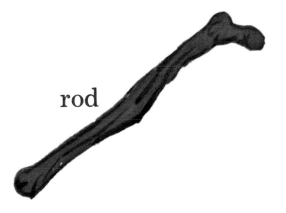
rod

sling

scroll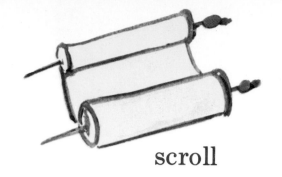

shepherd

Savior

salvation

sheep

sandals

1. If I had used a scroll, I would have
   a. read from it   b. walked on it
   c. worn it around my neck
2. When I hear about the Savior who can give me salvation, I hear about
   a. Jesus   b. the Angel Gabriel   c. Paul
3. If I had used sandals, I would have
   a. cooked dinner in them   b. worn them as shoes
4. If I had known a shepherd who took care of sheep, I would have seen him working
   a. in the city   b. in the suburbs   c. in the country
5. If I had used a sling, it would have been to
   a. hold up a broken arm   b. throw a stone   c. swing on it

1. If I had gone into a temple, it would have been to
     a. watch a ball game   b. worship God   c. roller skate
2. If I read the Ten Commandments, I would read something that
     a. Abraham wrote   b. Noah wrote   c. God wrote
3. If I had used a trumpet, I would have blown on it to
     a. make music or make a signal   b. play in an orchestra
4. If I had seen the tabernacle which Moses helped build, I would
   have seen
     a. a tent   b. a brick house   c. a house made of shingles
5. If I had watched by father thresh, I would have seen him
     a. drive a combine through a field
     b. drive cattle over wheat or barley, or beat the wheat or
        barley with something to get the grains from the heads

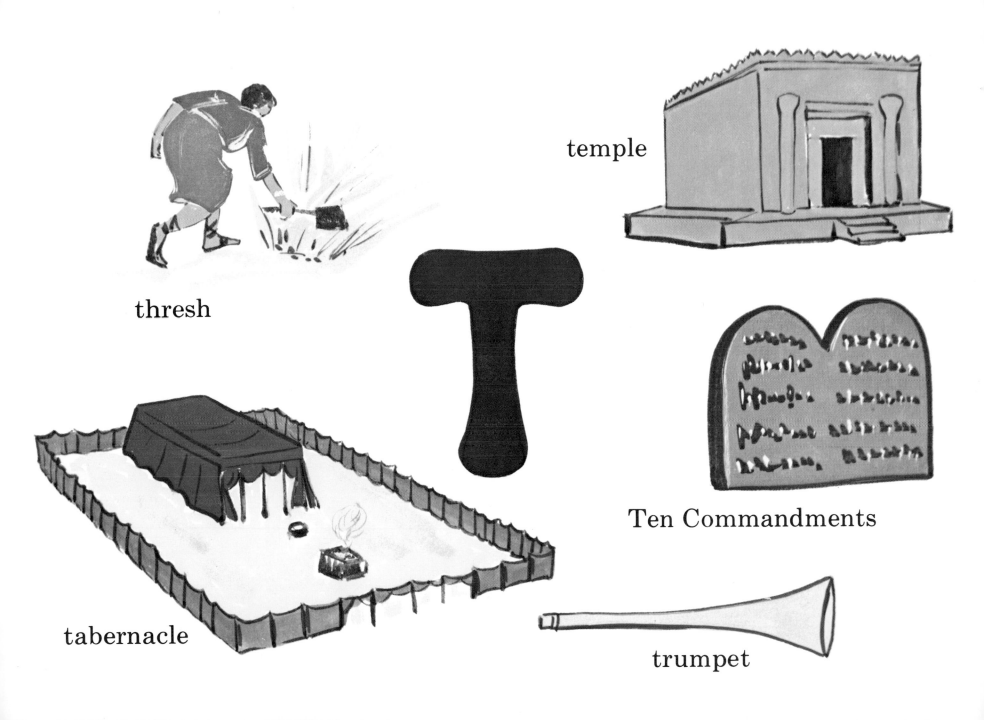

thresh

temple

tabernacle

Ten Commandments

trumpet

well

upper room

winnowing

U

V

W

watchtower

vineyard

Wise Men

1. If I had gone to an upper room with Jesus and His disciples, I might have seen them

      a. baptize people   b. eat the Last Supper   c. feed 5000 people

2. If I had seen one of the gifts the Wise Men gave Jesus, I would have seen

      a. silver   b. myrrh   c. cedar wood

3. If I had seen a man in a watchtower, I would have known that he was

      a. guarding crops against men or animals

      b. trying to tell time

      c. making watches

4. If I had gone to a vineyard, I would have seen

      a. grapes   b. vinegar bushes   c. vines with olives on them

5. If my father had been winnowing grain, he would have been

      a. selling grain at the market

      b. throwing grain into the air to get the chaff out

6. If my mother had taken water from a well, she would have

      a. turned on a faucet   b. pumped it up with an iron pump

      c. put a jar down into the well and pulled up the water

1. If my father had been Zacharias, I would have been
    a. Moses
    b. Peter
    c. John the Baptist
2. If I had seen a yoke, I would have seen it
    a. in an egg
    b. holding two oxen together
    c. in a yoke book
3. If I had seen Zacchaeus in a tree, it would have been
    a. an oak tree
    b. an olive tree
    c. a sycamore tree

Zacchaeus

Y

X

Z

Zacharias

yoke

ANSWER A BIBLE QUESTION

Every question needs an answer. You will find below an answer to each question in this book. But you will find more. You will find why Bible-time people did what they did. Or you may find more about the way they did something. If you like to think about Bible questions, you will also like to think about Bible answers.

A

1b and c. Noah had at least two of each kind of animal on the ark, so he would have had an antelope and an ape. But airplanes and ambulances had not been made yet.

2c. Alms were gifts or help for poor people.

3a. There were no apartment buildings or house trailers. Many people lived in tents.

4b. An adder was probably a poisonous snake.

5c. God had told His people to worship Him by burning meat on an altar. Since Jesus came, we do not worship God this way. Jesus gave us new ways to tell God we love Him.

6c. Angels did special work for God. We do not know if they had wings or not.

B

1c. People sewed the skins of goats around the edges. The hair was left on the outside. They put milk or water in these skins. Some jars made of baked clay were used as bottles. People in Egypt made little glass bottles, but not to drink from.

2b. Bible-time people did not have the big wooden barrel which we use today. They did not have much wood. It was easier to make a big jar.

3a. Benjamin and Joseph were Jacob's sons.

4c. Jesus was born in Bethlehem.

5b. When Moses was a baby, his mother put him into a basket made of bulrushes. People also made paper from bulrushes, sometimes called papyrus.

6b. There were no cardboard boxes as we know them.

C

1b. The word candle really means lamp. These little clay lamps burned night and day. Wax candles had not been made in Bible times. Even if they had, they would have melted in the hot weather of Bible lands.

2a. Bible-time people did not measure things by feet and inches. They did not have rulers, yardsticks, or tape measures. A cubit, about 18 inches, was the length of a man's arm from his elbow to his fingertips.

3a. Cavalry means men who fight on horses. Jesus died at Calvary.

4b. Oxen were too slow. Trucks and motors were made many years later.

5c. What we call corn did not grow in Bible lands at that time. The word corn meant any grain, especially wheat or barley.

6c. A centurion was an important man in Jesus' time because Romans ruled the country.

DE

1a. People got about 16¢ for a day's work then. But everything cost much less in Bible times.

2a. Decalogue is another name for the Ten Commandments.

3b. Very few dogs were kept as pets. Most dogs ran wild in the streets.

4a. A disciple was a person who followed what another person thought or did.

5a. Printing had not been invented in Bible times. Instead of books, these people used scrolls, long strips of papyrus wound on two sticks.

6a. See II Timothy 1: 5.

7b. Joseph and Noah were both dead at that time.

F

1a. Frankincense was a dried piece of resin from a certain kind of tree. When it was ground into powder and burned, it gave a good smell.

2b. Men wore these little pouches when they prayed in the morning.

3a. Fetters were put on prisoners.

4b. Israel had no flag in Bible times.

5b. Ten gallons is a lot of milk to drink!

6a. A farthing was a small Roman coin worth less than a cent.

7b. A fan was something like our pitchfork. Men threw grain into the air with it so the wind could blow away the chaff.

G

1b. A mirror was called a "glass" in the Bible. It was made of polished bronze. Glass as we know it today was not used much by the Hebrews.

2b. David fought the giant without armor. He was probably a teenager at the time.

3b. Grain was put between two big stones. One stone turned and ground the grain.

4a. A man who owned a field let others go after the harvesters and pick up the stalks of grain they missed.

5c. Romans and Greeks were Gentiles. Most Gentiles in Bible times did not worship God.

6a. The Gospel is very good news, for Jesus made a way for us to get to Heaven by believing in Him as our Savior.

HI

1b. Most horns were from animals. Some horns had a small hole cut in the sharp end so men could blow on them. Others were used to hold oil.

2a. An idol was usually a statue. Some people thought an idol was a god.

3a. Several rulers were called Herod. One Herod tried to kill the baby Jesus. Another Herod killed John the Baptist. Another killed James, the brother of John.

4b. Houses were not made of wood because there was not enough wood for everyone. Window glass and steel had not been made yet. Most houses were made of stones or mud bricks.

5b. Hamburgers were not made and sold in Bible times. Inns were like motels, a place to "park a camel" and sleep.

6c. God heard Hannah's prayers for a baby. He sent Samuel to be her child.

7c. A harp was a musical instrument with strings.

JK

1b. A javelin was a spear.

2a. Jews, or Hebrews, were Israelites. They were members of Abraham's family, but through his grandson Jacob. God gave Jacob a new name, Israel.

3b. This word is used only in the Old Testament.

4a. Sometimes this bowl was called a store. It was a bowl in which women mixed bread dough and let it rise before baking it.

5b. Jesus is our Savior because He save us from our sins when we ask Him.

6b and c. A kinsman was usually a relative. But sometimes he may have been a close friend, doing the things a relative would do.

L

1a. God had told His people to do this as a way to worship Him.

2b. A leper had a disease called leprosy. Many people thought he would give the disease to them. Sometimes he had to live away from others.

3b. Locusts could eat whole fields of crops.

4a. The Last Supper was the last meal Jesus ate with His disciples before He died on the cross.

5b. A latchet was a strap or leather strip which held a sandal on a foot.

6c. A lamp was a small clay dish with olive oil in it. People kept a lamp lit at all times.

M

1c. Grain was placed between two millstones. One turned on the other, grinding the grain.

2a. The mite was worth much less than a cent.

3a. Manna was called bread. It was more like bread than french fries or roast beef. Some people say it was more like seeds. God sent manna to feed His people in the wilderness.

4c. A manger was the trough from which an animal ate his food.

5a. A mantle was a piece of clothing, usually a cloak.

6c. The word Messiah meant the same as the word Christ. Just as kings were chosen to do a special work, Jesus was chosen to do God's special work.

N

1a. Naaman was a leper. Elisha healed him, with God's help.

2c. Noah built the ark, or big boat.

3b. Jesus grew up at Nazareth. Isaac and Abraham did not.

4a. Chronicles and Psalms are in the Old Testament.

5a. Nicodemus went to see Jesus one night. He and Jesus talked about the way to go to Heaven.

O

1c. Almost all the oil in Bible times came from olives. Oil wells were not drilled then. There were no filling stations.

2b. There have always been many olive trees in Bible lands.

3b. Some jars were made this size to help people get the right amount.

4c. People then did not have electricity or gas.

5a. Philemon and Jude are New Testament books.

6b. Boxes with tubes that looked like trumpets were on a wall in the temple. There were no collection plates passed.

P

1a. Pottage was a thick vegetable soup with meat added. The vegetables were often lentils, something like split peas.

2b. A plumb line was a string with a stone or piece of metal at the bottom. This held the string straight up and down. It helped a man know if his wall was straight.

3b. A penny was another name for the coin called a denarius. It was worth about 16^e. A man had to work all day to earn one coin.

4c. People in Israel did not have many horses. Oxen were used for plowing. There were no tractors then.

5b. Pharisees sometimes owned sheep, but they did not work as shepherds. Most Pharisees did not like Jesus. They thought He was not God's Son. They did not like it when He told them that He was.

6c. A prophet was God's helper. He told people about God.

QR

1c. A rabbi was usually a teacher. He taught the rules that God gave. He also taught the rules the religious leaders made.

2a. A shepherd used a rod to fight wild animals who tried to hurt his sheep. Sometimes he used a rod to help him walk.

3c. The Romans ruled the land of Israel during the time of Jesus. Most of the Jews hated them.

4b. People who fought or hunted with bows and arrows carried a quiver. It was a case which held the arrows.

5c. Esther was a queen. Ruth and Hannah were not.

S

1a. People in Bible times did not have the kind of books we have. Instead, they had scrolls. A scroll was a long piece of papyrus (see bulrushes), or animal skins, rolled on two sticks.

2a. Jesus is the only Savior. He is the only One who can save us from our sins.

3b. Sandals were one kind of Bible-time shoes. They were made of hard leather. Other kinds of Bible-time shoes were made of soft leather.

4c. Shepherds kept their sheep in the country so they could eat grass and plants.

5b. A sling in Bible times was something like a sling shot today. But it did not have a Y-shaped stick. It was a long strip of leather with a pocket in the middle. A stone was put in the pocket. A person held both ends of the leather strip and whirled it round and round. When the sling went fast enough, the person let one end of it go. This sent the stone flying toward its mark.

T

1b. A temple was something like our church. It was a building where people went to pray and give money to God.

2c. The Bible says that God wrote the Ten Commandments with His finger.

3a. There were no orchestras as we know them in Bible lands.

4a. The tabernacle was a big tent.

5b. There were no combines. To get the grains of wheat or barley from the heads, men beat them with big sticks or drove cattle over them.

UVW

1b. Jesus and His disciples ate The Last Supper in an upper room. An upper room was the second or third floor.

2b. The three kinds of gifts were gold, frankincense, and myrrh.

3a. A watchtower was a stone tower where a watchman stayed while crops were growing.

4a. A vineyard had grape vines in it. There are no vinegar bushes. Olives grow on trees.

5b. When the chaff blew away, the grain would fall down to the ground. When all the chaff was gone, the grain could be put in sacks. Later it would be ground into flour.

6c. People did not have faucets, pumps, or water pipes which we have today. They tied a rope to a jar and let it down into a well.

XYZ

1c. Elizabeth was the mother of John the Baptist.

2b. A yoke was a big piece of wood which held two oxen together. This made the oxen pull at the same time.

3c. When Zacchaeus wanted to see Jesus, he climbed into a sycamore tree.